HOW THE CROSS BECAME A SWORD

RICHARD BOOKER

How the Cross Became a Sword

Copyright © 1994 by Sounds of the Trumpet, Inc.

All rights reserved. No portion of this booklet may be reproduced without prior written permission from the author.

Printed in the United States of America

ISBN 0-9615302-3-5

Cover Design by Michael Washer

Table of Contents

Preface ... The First Jewish Revolt ... The Second Jewish Revolt ... The Emergence of Rabbinical Judaism ... Gentile Christianity ... A Greek World View ... Statements From The Early Church Fathers ... The Writings Of Augustine ... The "Christ-Killers" ... The Allegorical Interpretation Of Scripture ... Origen And The School At Alexandria ... The Paganization Of Christianity ... The Crusades ... Anti-Semitism ... The Inquisition ... The Russian Pogroms ... The Holocaust ... Anti-Zionism ... The Christian Response ... References ... Book Order Form ... Tape Order Form

Preface

In the fourth century, a man named John Chrysostom (344 A.D.-407 A.D.) was the bishop of the Church of Antioch. He was a great orator. In fact his name means, "Golden-Mouthed." He had tremendous influence and is considered one of the greatest of the early church Fathers.

But John Chrysostom had a problem - he hated Jews. He blamed the entire Jewish race for the death of Jesus and sought to separate Christianity from its Jewish roots.

John Chrysostom gave a series of eight sermons in which he spoke violently against the Jews. His sermons were put in written form and widely circulated. Although many early church Fathers spoke harshly against the Jews, John Chrysotom was the most vicious. His sermons fanned the flames of anti-Semitism that became the official teaching and practice of the church for the next 1,600 years.

The *Jewish-Christian Relations Series* was written to refute and rebuke the writings of John Chrysostom. It was written to express love to the Jewish people, to call the church to repentance for its anti-Semitic past and to help the church understand God's eternal purposes for the Jewish people and the nation of Israel.

The sermons given by John Chrysostom began a legacy of hate towards the Jewish people that is still with us today. *The Jewish-Christian Relations Series* was written with the hope that it will cause a new beginning of love and understanding between Christians and Jews.

You may order additional copies of this booklet and other relevant materials by using the Order Form in the back of this publication. SHALOM!

How the Cross Became a Sword

I recently met a Jewish woman who acknowledged Jesus as her Messiah. When she shared her beliefs with a relative, the relative responded, "Jews don't believe that Jesus is the Messiah because Christians hate us."

Of course many Jews do believe in Jesus as their Messiah, and not all Christians hate Jews. But the relative's statement expressed the tragic history of Jewish-Christian relations for the past 1,800 years.

It was with this knowledge of the hate shown by the Christian church towards the Jews that Adolf Hitler was able to write in Mein Kampf, "Hence today I believe that I am acting in accordance with the Almighty Creator: by defending myself against the Jew, I am fighting for the work of the Lord" (Adolf Hitler, *Mein Kampf,* translated by Ralph Manheim (Boston:Houghton Mifflin Co. 1971), page 65).

How did a movement that began as a sect of Judaism with a Jewish Savior establish such a legacy of hatred towards the Jewish people? How did the cross, God's symbol of love, become a sword, the church's symbol of hate?

The two basic contributing factors to this tragedy were the separation of Christianity from its Jewish roots followed by the Gentile acceptance and paganization of Christianity. How this happened is the subject of this booklet. I pray that God will use this information to help bring reconciliation between Christians and Jews as the time is now for us to bind our hearts together in spite of our differences.

How the Cross Became a Sword

The First Jewish Revolt

A number of events separated Christianity from its Jewish roots and sowed the seeds of anti-Semitism in the first three centuries of the church.

The first of these events was the *First Jewish Revolt* initiated by the Zealots in 66 A.D. It ended in 73 A.D. with the fall of Masada where 967 Zealots took their own lives rather than being taken by the Romans.

The Zealots were nationalistic-minded Jews who hated the Romans and wanted to drive them out of Israel. They had considerable influence among the common people and were waiting for an opportune moment to rally them against the Romans.

When the Roman Governor, Florus, attacked the Jews, Elazar, the High Priest of the Temple, stopped offering the daily sacrifice on behalf of the emperor's health. This was the moment for which the Zealots had been waiting. They quickly moved against the Romans.

The Roman General, Flavius Vespasian, began to put down the revolt in Galilee, but he was called to Rome and made emperor at the death of Nero in 68 A.D. His son, Titus, took command and destroyed Jerusalem and the Jewish Temple in 70 A.D.

Titus had 80,000 well-seasoned Roman soldiers at his command. The siege lasted six months and ended on the 9th of Av (July-August). Ironically, this was the same date Nebuchadnezzar destroyed Solomon's Temple in 586 B.C. (Jeremiah 39:2).

Approximately one million Jews died in this siege of Jerusalem. Many of the survivors were sold as slaves to foreign merchants who carried them off to the various nations of the world. This was certainly one of the greatest tragedies in the history of the Jewish people.

Prior to this catastrophe, Jerusalem was the center of worship for Judaism and Christianity. The Jewish believers were a constant witness to both Jews and Gentiles regarding the "Jewishness" of Jesus and Christianity.

However, when it became clear that the Romans were going to attack Jerusalem, many of the Jewish believers fled the city and took refuge in Pella, a city located about 60 miles northeast of Jerusalem. They did not flee because they were cowards deserting their Jewish brethren. They fled because Jesus had instructed them to do so.

Jesus prophesied the destruction of Jerusalem and told His followers, "But when you see Jerusalem surrounded by armies, then know that its desolation is near. Then let those who are in Judea flee to the mountains, let those who are in the midst of her depart, and let not those who are in the country enter her" (Luke 21:20-21).

According to Eusebius in *The History of the Church* (page 156), there were fifteen bishops of the church (all Jewish) who either stayed in Jerusalem or returned from

Pella. They guided the church from the time of James (Acts 15) to the Second Jewish Revolt.

The surviving Jewish community considered them to be traitors. *And since many of the Jewish believers were no longer in Jerusalem, Christianity was not as clearly perceived as a sect of Judaism.* Thus began a major separation of the Jewish believers from their non-believing Jewish brethren. Furthermore, with the destruction of Jerusalem, Gentile cities would become the center of the Christian faith. Jerusalem would no longer be considered the "Mother-City" of Christianity.

The Second Jewish Revolt

Another major event that separated Christianity from its Jewish roots was the *Second Jewish Revolt.* You would think that the horrible devastation and destruction by the Romans would have broken the Jewish will to resist. But it didn't! A new hope for freedom arose a generation later. This hope was in the form of a would-be military messiah by the name of Simon Bar Kochba. Simon Bar Kochba claimed to be the deliverer who would overthrow the Roman yoke of bondage.

This freedom fighter led the Jewish people in another great war of revolt against the Romans in 132 A.D. He was aided in his quest by the honored Rabbi Akiba who convinced the struggling Zealots that Bar Kochba was the

How the Cross Became a Sword

Messiah. In fact, it was Rabbi Akiba who gave Simon the name "Bar Kochba" which means "Son of a Star." This is a Messianic title from the book of Numbers (Numbers 24:17).

The revolt lasted three years but was crushed in 135 A.D. by the Roman emperor Hadrian. Hadrian butchered the Jews unmercifully. More than half a million perished. He completely destroyed Jerusalem and constructed a temple to Jupiter on the site of the Jewish Temple.

The Jews who survived were sold as slaves to the same foreign merchants who had earlier carried off their parents. Jerusalem was declared off- limits to the Jews. As a further insult to the Jews, Hadrian renamed the land of Israel after their ancient enemy the Philistines. He called it *Palestine*! He renamed Jerusalem in honor of both himself (Hadrian Aelius) and the temple of Jupiter at Rome on Capitoline hill. He called Jerusalem "Aelia Capitalina."

The Second Jewish Revolt was not only a disaster for the Jewish people, but it also was significant in widening the separation between the Jewish believers and the larger Jewish community. Once again, the Jewish believers refused to fight. They could not support the revolt because of the Messianic claims of Bar Kochba.

The Jewish believers acknowledged Jesus as the Messiah. They could not, therefore, follow Bar Kochba. Even though Rabbi Akiba acknowledged a *false Messiah*, he was greatly honored while the Jewish believers were again labeled as traitors. The fact that the Jewish leadership supported Bar Kochba was a signal to the Jewish believers of their final rejection of Jesus as the Messiah. It's ironic that later rabbinical teachings sought to discredit Bar Kochba. They referred to him as "Bar Kosba" which means, "Son of Lies."

The Emergence of Rabbinical Judaism

A third happening that separated Christianity from its Jewish roots was the emergence of *Rabbinical Judaism.*

The Jewish religious leaders who survived the First Jewish Revolt assembled at Yavneh, a small town located near the modern city of Joppa. These religious leaders belonged to the Pharisaic sect of Judaism. Their purpose for assembling was to restructure Judaism so that it could survive without the very essence of its faith; the temple, sacrifices for atonement and priesthood. The Sandhedrin (Jewish Supreme Council) also convened at Yavneh.

The strategy for survival was to form an academy (theological center) where the rabbis would develop and teach their restructured Judaism.

There were two leading Pharisaic schools at this time, and they competed against each other. The School of Shammai had a highly nationalistic, pro-revolutionary view. Today we would think of them as right-wing fundamentalists who kept to a very strict interpretation of Jewish laws and traditions. The school of Hillel was more moderate. The rabbis decided that the teachings of the School of Hillel would form the basic foundation on which to rebuild their restructured Judaism.

One significance of this was that Rabbinical Judaism would focus less on looking for a Messianic deliverer while Jewish believers, and later Gentile Christians, hoped for the soon return of Jesus.

A pupil of Hillel, Johonan ben Zakkai was the first head of the Academy of Yavneh. He was a realist who recognized the need to change in order to establish a Judaism that could survive in a post-Temple era.

For example, when a student asked Rabbi Zakkai how they could seek atonement without a sacrifice, he replied that good deeds would take the place of sacrifices.

Rabbinical Judaism, out of necessity, was to become a religion of works, whereas Christianity would emphasize atonement through the sacrificial death of Jesus.

Rabbinical Judaism would emphasize rules for living in this present world. Christianity would emphasize a personal relationship with Jesus as the "Living Torah" and focus on life in the hereafter.

While Rabbi Zakkai laid the foundation for Rabbinical Judaism, his successor, Rabban Gamaliel II (90-115) gave it prestige and acceptance. He is called "Rabban" rather than rabbi because of his status among the early Jewish sages.

His grandfather was Rabban Gamaliel who was a prominent leader of the Sanhedrin as described in the book of Acts. It was his wise counsel to the Sanhedrin that kept them from killing the disciples of Jesus. He said, "And now I say to you, keep away from these men and let them alone; for if this plan or this work is of men, it will come to nothing; but if it is of God, you cannot overthrow it lest you even be found to fight against God" (Acts 5:38-39).

According to Acts 22:3, Rabban Gamaliel had an outstanding student who was also destined for greatness. His name was Saul, later called Paul, the apostle of Jesus Christ.

Rabban Gamaliel's father was also a highly regarded leader prior to the destruction of the Temple in 70 A.D.

It is believed that during the time of Rabban Gamaliel's leadership, the boundaries of Rabbinical Judaism were established and a prayer of condemnation was given against any Jews whose beliefs did not conform to the norm established by the rabbis. As a result, Jewish believers in Jesus were considered heretics and excluded from the rabbinical religious community. Unfortunately, this act formally separated the synagogue and the church.

Later in the second century, the center of Rabbinical Judaism was relocated from Yavneh to Tiberias. It was then that Rabbi Judah the Prince collected the "Jewish Oral Law" and put it in written form. This written collection was called the *Mishna*. It was completed around 220 A.D.

The rabbis taught that when God gave Moses the Written Law, He also gave the Jewish people an Oral Law, or tradition, to guide them in living by the Written Law. As a result, the rabbis considered the Oral Law to be Sacred Scriptures along with the Written Law.

The Oral Law was committed to memory and passed from rabbi to student. However, with the Jews being dispersed among the nations, it became important to document the Oral Law.

The Mishna is a book of laws that became the foundational document of Rabbinical Judaism from the time it was written to our day.

The rabbis added the Mishna to the Tanakh (Old Testament) based on their oral traditions. The Christians added the New Testament based on the life and of Jesus and the teachings of the apostles.

To summarize, Christianity was separated from its Jewish roots as a result of the First and Second Jewish revolts and the emergence of Rabbinical Judaism. Because of these events, the center of Christianity moved from Jerusalem to Gentile cities. The followers of Jesus were considered traitors and heretics who were to lose much of their Jewish identity. Judaism and Christianity added two different books to their Sacred Scriptures, thus going separate ways.

Gentile Christianity

The second basic contributing factor to Christian anti-Semitism was the acceptance and paganization of Christianity by the Gentiles. There were four major developments.

A Greek World View

The first was the *Greek world view* of the early church Fathers.

As previously mentioned, Christianity began as a sect of Judaism. In fact, the early Christians were known as Nazarenes.

Jesus (Yeshua in Hebrew) was born into a Jewish family and lived His entire life as an observant Jew. His followers were Jewish. They worshipped on Saturday, attended Synagogue and kept the feasts. They acknowledged Jesus as the Jewish Messiah and wrote the New Testament Scriptures.

The Jewish believers in Jesus were successful in spreading their message to the Gentiles. In a way, they were too successful. The Gentiles became the leaders of this new Christian faith.

For the most part, these Gentile Christian leaders had little regard for Jewish people. *Many of them taught Greek philosophy and brought a Greek world view into the church.* They lacked the necessary Hebraic background that would have helped them keep the church connected to its Jewish roots. Although they accepted Jesus in their heart, Plato ruled their mind.

Furthermore, their attempt to merge Greek philosophy with the Tanakh resulted in their adopting teachings and perceptions that were often more Greek oriented than Jewish. This means they were not biblical!

For example, the Bible teaches that God created a world that was good for our enjoyment (Gen. 1:31). Although the world has been cursed by sin, we are to experience the grace of God in this world and express His grace in our lives to our community by works of loving kindness. The primary structure ordained by God for expressing His grace was, and still is, marriage and the family. *We were to bless God for all things that were good and worship Him with our body, soul and spirit in this present world.*

Plato taught that the physical or material world was bad. In view of this, he presented the idea that we should be otherworldly minded and seek escape from this world. While Jesus said, "The meek shall inherit the earth" (Matt. 5:3), Plato could have led the church choir in singing, "This old world is not my home, I'm just a passing through." Although Jesus said, "Go into the world and make disciples" (Matt. 28:19), the Gentile church adopted Platonic philosophy and retreated to the monastery.

God said, "It is not good that man should be alone" (Gen. 2:18). But the church viewed marriage as an inferior way of life and glorified celibacy. Instead of priests marrying and raising godly families, they became monks in order to deny the sinful desires of the flesh. To be spiritual was to be single and miserable.

Whereas the Bible says, "Whatever you do, do it as unto the Lord" (Col 3:23), the church made a division between the sacred and the secular. The sacred was what happened in the church building on Sunday while everything else was secular. As a result, people were to act "spiritual" on Sunday, while free to live for themselves the rest of the week.

Salvation became a way of escape from the evils of this world rather than the means of redeeming the world.

Instead of being kingdom conscious, the church became heaven conscious. Faith became a matter of right thinking rather than right acting. Words, doctrines and religious creeds soon replaced deeds for righteous living.

Christianity became solely a personal matter rather than a corporate expression of people living out their faith as a covenant community. Rather than blessing God for His goodness, the church chose to bless things such as dead food on a plate.

This Greek way of perceiving the world has influenced church doctrines and practices since the second century and been a major cause of Christian anti-Semitism. This is because humans have a tendency to view with scorn those whose attitudes and ways are different from theirs.

Statements From The Church Fathers

Because of this Greek influence in their lives and the lack of a Hebraic perspective of the Bible, most of the early church Fathers were very anti-Semitic in their thinking. They expressed this through their speeches and writings which were highly negative and inflammatory concerning the Jews.

For example, *Justin Martyr* (100 A.D.-165 A.D.) claimed that God's covenant with the Jews was no longer valid and that Gentiles had replaced Jews in God's redemptive plan.

Ignatius, who was the bishop of the church at Antioch early in the second century, wrote that anyone who celebrated the Passover with the Jews, or received emblems of the Jewish feast, was a partaker with those that killed the Lord and His apostles.

Tertullian (160 A.D.-220 A.D.) was one of the most important Christian writers of the second century. His works were highly significant in developing the basic doctrines of the church. In one of his writings called,

Against the Jews, he blamed the entire Jewish race for the death of Jesus.

Clement of Alexandria (150 A.D.-215 A.D.) emphasized Greek philosophy rather than the Tanakh as the primary means God gave the Gentiles to lead them to Jesus as the ultimate "Word of God."

Origen (185 A.D.-253 A.D.) accused the Jews of plotting to kill Christians.

Eusebius (263 A.D.-339 A.D.) wrote the history of the church for the first three centuries. He taught that the promises and blessings in the Tanakh were for the Christians and that the curses were for the Jews. He declared the church was the "true Israel of God" that had replaced literal Israel in God's covenants.

John Chrysostom (344 A.D.-407 A.D.) was the bishop of the church at Antioch and the greatest preacher of his day. He gave a series of eight sermons in which he spoke violently against the Jews. He said there could never be forgiveness for the Jews and that God had always hated them. He taught it was the "Christian duty" to hate the Jews. According to Chrysostom, the Jews were the assassins of Christ and worshipers of the devil.

Chrysostom preached, "The synagogue is worse than a brothel ... It is the den of scoundrels ... the temple of demons devoted to idolatrous cults ... a place of meeting for the assassins of Christ ... a house worse than a drinking shop ... a den of thieves; a house of ill fame, a dwelling of iniquity, the refuge of devils, a gulf and abyss of perdition ... As for me, I hate the synagogue ... I hate the Jews for the same reason." (Malcolm Hay, *The Roots of Christian Anti-Semitism* (New York: Liberty Press, 1981), pages 27-28.)

Jerome (345 A.D.-420 A.D.) was a great Bible scholar. His Latin translation of the Scriptures became the official Bible of the church. Jerome claimed that the Jews were incapable of understanding the Scriptures and that they should be severely persecuted until they confess the "true faith."

All of the writers of the Bible believed that a Jewish Messiah would establish a literal kingdom on the earth. Messiah would rule over this kingdom from a literal restored Jerusalem for a literal period of 1,000 years. During the Messiah's rule, a literal restored Israel would be the head nation of the world. The blessings of this literal kingdom of God would come to the Gentiles through the literal nation of Israel as they live under the literal rule of the Messiah who would literally sit on the literal throne of David.

This "literal" interpretation of Scripture was not compatible with the replacement theology teaching of the church as the kingdom of God. Although there are two realms to the kingdom of God, one literal and the other spiritual, the church chose to completely ignore the literal realm and accepted only the spiritual realm. This was because the spiritualizing of the kingdom was the only way the church fathers could establish their theology that the church was the true Israel that had replaced literal Israel.

The church, in partnership with the Christian Emperor, would establish the spiritual kingdom of God in the hearts of mankind throughout the world.

The Writings Of Augustine

Augustine (354 A.D.-430 A.D.) was the theologian who explained this new interpretation of Scripture for the church and the world. In his work, *The City of God*, Augustine used Origen's allegorical method of interpreting the Scriptures and spiritualized the relationship between the church and the Jews for events relating to the end-times and the kingdom of God. He wrote that the Millennial kingdom of God was not literal but spiritual. He taught that the kingdom of God was present and not future and existed only in the spiritual sense in the hearts of men.

If you accept Augustine's writings, you believe that you are now living in the millennial kingdom of God on earth, which is the church, as a citizen of the New Jerusalem, which is spiritual. The devil is effectively bound, and you are establishing God's rule over the earth. When you have conquered the world for God, Jesus will come to earth and eternity will begin.

If you believe this fairy tale, I'd like to sell you some PLO resort property in the Gaza Strip.

This triumphant view of the church was manifested by Christian dominance of the Jews who were to be forever humiliated and disgraced as poor slaves to their Christian masters.

Augustine wrote that the Jews deserved death, but instead, they were destined to wander the earth as a witness to their punishment and the victory of the church over the synagogue. The greater their humiliation, the greater the triumph of the church.

Augustine's writings became the theological textbook for the church, and his views are still taught today by much of the Christian world. No wonder anti-Semitism is rampant in the church.

Thank God that the Catholic church has finally acknowledged the error of this teaching and formally refuted much of it.

The "Christ-Killers"

A second significant development within Gentile Christianity was that the church Fathers blamed the entire race of Jewish people for the death of Jesus. They did not understand there was no "one Jewish voice" which spoke for the entire nation.

In the first century, the Jews were divided into five major sects or movements. These were the Sadducees, the Pharisees, the Zealots, the Essenes and the Jewish Christians (Messianic Jews).

The *Sadducees* were the priests who controlled and administered sacrificial worship at the Temple. Since Temple worship was the most important element of Jewish life in Jerusalem, the Sadducees were very powerful. They were basically the "upper-class" aristocratic group who were comfortable living in a Greek-Roman world. In view of their influence and power, they were suspicious of any activity that might threaten their position. The destruction of the Temple in 70 A.D. brought an end to the Sadducees.

The second major sect was the *Pharisees*. They were basically the "middle-class" group. They were not comfortable living in a Greek-Roman world and identified with the common people. Whereas the Sadducees had the pocketbooks of the masses, the Pharisees had their hearts.

The Pharisees were the primary teachers of the Tanakh and the Oral Law. Unlike the Sadducees, they were not politicians but religious leaders held in high regard by the people. Because of their emphasis on the Bible, tradition and the synagogue, they survived the destruction by the Romans and established the Rabbinical form of Judaism at Yavneh. It was this Judaism that laid the foundation for Jewish faith and practice in the centruies that would follow.

A third Jewish sect was the *Zealots*. As mentioned previously, the Zealots were a nationalistic minded sect that desired to overthrow the Roman by force. They were revolutionaries who died in the First and Second Jewish Revolts. It was members of this group who committed mass suicide at Masada.

Another Jewish sect was the *Essenes*. The Essenes were an ascetic group that, some believe, established the community at Qumran and wrote the Dead Sea Scrolls. The Romans destroyed this community in 68 A.D.

The *Jewish Christians* (Messianic Believers) survived the First and Second Revolts. However, being in exile, their movement soon lost its Jewish discinctiveness and evolved into a Gentile Christianity that was cut off from its Jewish roots.

So who actually killed Jesus? The biblical record is clear. God himself initiated Jesus' death as the atonement for our sins, Jew and Gentile.

The prophet Isaiah wrote of Jesus, "Surely He has borne our griefs and carried our sorrows; yet we esteemed Him stricken, smitten by God, and affllicted. But He was woulded for our trangressions, He was bruised for our iniquities; the chastisement for our peace was upon Him and by His stripes we are healed" (Is. 53:4-5).

How the Cross Became a Sword

Jesus also had a part in His own death. He willingly gave His life as the sacrifice for our sins. Isaiah further wrote, "He was oppressed and He was afflicted, yet He opened not His mouth; He was led as a lamb to the slaughter, and as a sheep before its shearers is silent, so He opened not His mouth" (Is. 53:7).

Jesus must have been thinking about Isaiah's words when He said, "Therefore My Father loves Me, because I lay down My life that I may take it up again. No one takes it from Me, but I lay it down of Myself. I have power to lay it down and I have power to take it again. This command I have received from My Father" (John 10:17-18).

In God's calendar of time, the ethnic people that actually crucified Jesus were the Jews and Romans. But it wasn't all the Jews and all the Romans that crucified Jesus. To the contrary, many Jews acknowledged Jesus as the Messiah while most Romans never even heard of Jesus at the time of His death.

Jesus' life and ministry brought about a tremendous spiritual revival among the Jewish people. His words and deeds gave hope to the common people who followed Him by the thousands. The crowds were so large, Jesus had to make a determined effort to get away from them. (See Mark 2:45; 3:7-9).

Although many in the crowds were merely curiosity seekers, a significant number believed in Jesus as the

How the Cross Became a Sword

Messiah. In fact so many Jewish people were following Jesus, He became a threat to the established leadership who carefully watched anyone who was drawing a crowd.

It was a small group of religious and political leaders who desired to crucify Jesus becuase they were jealous of His fame and afraid He would upset their comfortable relationship with the Romans.

John wrote, "Then the chief priests and the Pharisees gathered a council and said, 'What shall we do? For this man works many signs. If we let Him alone like this, everyone will believe in Him and the Romans will come and take away both our place and nation.' And one of them, Caiaphas, being the high priest that year, said to them, 'You know nothing at all, nor do you consider that it is expedient for us that one man should die for the people and not that the whole nation should perish' ... then from that day on, they plotted to put Him to death" (John 11:47-50,53).

Mark wrote that Pilate knew the religious leaders handed Jesus over to him because of envy (Mark 15:9-10).

Gentile Roman authority and Roman soldiers actually crucified Jesus. Pilate knew that Jesus had done nothing to deserve death. But he was a weak administrator who crucified Jesus at the insistence of the chief priest who stirred up a mob to frighten and intimidate Pilate to go along with their wishes.

Luke wrote, "But they were insistent, demanding with loud voices that He be crucified. And the voices of these men and of the chief priests prevailed. So Pilate gave sentence that it should be as they requested" (Luke 23:23-24).

God could have just as easily chosen any other ethnic group to crucify Jesus. It could have been the Americans, the French, the PLO, the Russians, Germans, British, Chinese, etc. He chose the Jews and Romans to fulfill the prophetic Scriptures. Instead of hating them, we should hate sin because it is sin that separates us from God and crucified Jesus.

Because of God's love, He allowed Jesus to pay the price of sin for us so that we don't have to pay it ourselves. As Isaiah wrote, "All we like sheep have gone astray; we have turned, everyone, to his own way; and the LORD has laid on Him the iniquity of us all" (Is. 53:6).

Jews and Gentiles should put away their stones and love one another in spite of their differences. We don't have to agree on the identity of the Messiah to love one another.

The Allegorical Interpretation Of Scripture

One of the most important concerns in understanding the Bible is how to interpret the Bible. This leads us to the next difficulty between the early church and the Jews.

A third major development in Gentile Christianity was the acceptance of the *allegorical method* of interpreting the Bible.

There are certain principles or rules we must follow in order to properly interpret the Bible. One of the most important of these principles is to interpret the Bible in its literal sense unless the context indicates otherwise.

There are certain types of statements in the Bible that we should not interpret literally. These are called "figurative statements." A figurative statement is used to communicate something other than the statement's normal, literal meaning. But unless the biblical context clearly indicates otherwise, we should interpret the Bible literally as it is written. To do otherwise can lead one to serious misunderstanding of the Scriptures.

Unfortunately, the early church Fathers did not follow this important principle of literal interpretation. Instead they spiritualized or allegorized much of what they read. This was particularly true regarding the Scriptures pertaining to the relationship between Israel and the church and the prophetic Scriptures that deal with end-time events. Here's how it happened.

Origen And The School At Alexandria

One of the most important cities of the first century was Alexandria, Egypt. Founded by Alexander the Great in

How the Cross Became a Sword

---

331 B.C., it was a major center of commerce and learning, having perhaps the greatest library of the ancient world.

Being a Greek city, it naturally had a Greek character and world view. Greek philosophy, science and literature and Greek methods of interpreting the Greek mysteries were taught at the university. *The Greek method of interpretation was allegorical.*

There was a school for the instruction of new Christians in Alexandria. It was the first theological school of Christendom. Because of the Greek culture at Alexandria, the Christian school of learning focused on merging Greek philosophy with Christianity by using the allegorical method of interpreting the Bible.

The first head of the school was a converted stoic philosopher named *Pantaenus* who became the chief instructor until about the year 180 A.D. His most famous student was *Clement* who succeeded Pantaenus and was head of the school until 202 A.D.

Clement was born in Athens to pagan parents. After converting to Christianity, he went to Alexandria to study under Pantaenus.

Clement blended Greek philosophy with Christianity in order to make Christianity acceptable to the Gentiles. He taught that God gave philosophy to the Greeks to lead them to Christ, the ultimate truth, just as He gave the Tanakh to the Jews to prepare them for the Messiah.

How the Cross Became a Sword

It seems that Clement was more comfortable with Plato than he was with Moses. As a result, Clement and his students looked more to Athens than they did Jerusalem. Clement laid the foundation built on by his successors which would emphasize Greek philosophy as the forerunner to Christianity, rather than the Tanakh. This would play a major role in severing the Jewish roots of Christianity.

Clement is best known for his famous pupil and successor, *Origen*. It is difficult to understand the significance and influence of Origen because there is no one comparable to him today. He was the greatest scholar of his time.

Origen was born in Egypt of Christian parents in about the year 185 A.D. His father suffered martyrdom in 202 A.D. Origen sought martyrdom as well but was restrained by his mother.

Origen was only eighteen when he became the head of the school in 203 A.D. He held this position for the next 27 years. He also established a school and great library in Caesarea.

Origen's knowledge of philosophy and theology were so great that people from all walks of life sought his counsel. His fame and influence was unparalleled being recognized throughout the Roman world even by the Emperor.

Origen taught the allegorical method of interpreting the Scriptures. As previously mentioned, the allegorical method of interpretation denies the literal meaning of the text. You can make the text mean anything you want it to mean which usually leads to speculative fantasies and conclusions that have no relationship to the true meaning of the text. Unfortunately, this is exactly what happened to Origen.

Origen looked for hidden meanings behind everything he read, including the Scriptures. Because he did not give proper consideration to the natural meaning of the text, he arrived at conclusions that grew from his own fertile imagination. Some of his interpretations and teachings were so absurd that many of his peers considered him to be a heretic. By today's standards, Origen would certainly not be considered an orthodox Christian. He was excommunicated on more than one occasion for his views.

Even though many of Origen's interpretations and teachings were rejected by friend and foe alike, his allegorical method of interpreting the Scriptures was accepted and became the standard. It is this system that produced the teaching that the church is the "New Israel" of God that has replaced literal Israel in the plan and purposes of God.

Origen literally interpreted the Scriptures that promised judgment and curses on Israel but applied the blessings spiritually to the church. In this way, Origen spiritualized the Tanakh making it acceptable to the church and the Gentile world.

Incidentally, one Scripture which Origen should have interpreted allegorically is Matthew 19:12 which reads, "... there are eunuchs who have made themselves eunuchs for the kingdom of heaven's sake. He who is able to accept it, let him accept it." Origen literally was able to accept it and castrated himself.

During the reign of Emperor Decius (244 A.D.-251 A.D.), thousands of Christians were martyred. Origen was a special case. He was tortured but not killed. After Decius died, Origen was released from prison and went to Tyre to live out his days and write his sermons. He died in peace in 253 A.D. at the age of sixty-nine.

As mentioned, Origen had established a theological school and library at Caesarea with the help of his friend and student Pamphilus. Before he died, Origen taught at the school, and many of his students became the leading theologians of the early church. Origen's students accepted his allegorical method of interpreting the Scriptures and established it as official church teaching. *This laid the foundation for anti-Semitism in the church that was built on by successive generations until the Puritan revival in the 1600's.*

Pamphilus became the chief instructor at the school in Caesarea where he taught Origen's views to his students.

His most important student was a man named *Eusebius* (263 A.D.-339 A.D.).

Eusebius was a great admirer of Origen and is considered the "Father of Church History." His most important writing, *Ecclesiastical History* is the only surviving account of the church during the first 300 years to the time of Constantine.

Eusebius became the bishop at Caesarea and later an intimate friend and advisor of the Emperor Constantine who embraced Christianity as the official religion of Rome around the year 312 A.D.

We will now see how Eusebius influenced Constantine with Origen's allegorical interpretation of Scriptures and anti-Semitic teachings.

The Paganization of Christianity

Constantine unified the Roman empire by converting it to the Christian religion. However, the struggling new religion itself was not united.

There were several major controversies that threatened to tear it apart. One controversy had to do with the proper date to celebrate Jesus' resurrection. Constantine, with Eusebius at his side, called for a church counsel to settle the issue.

The counsel of Nicea met in 325 A.D. It was decided that the church would celebrate the resurrection of Jesus on the Sunday following the first full moon after the vernal equinox (March 21) rather than on the biblical date. The Roman pagan calendar replaced the Jewish calendar and the Jewish feast of First Fruits, the resurrection feast, became Easter the spring festival when the pagans worshiped Ishtar.

The church not only changed the date of Jesus' resurrection, they also changed the date of His crucifixion from Passover to Good Friday.

The Romans worshiped many gods, but their high god was the Sun. Their great winter festival was on December 25 which the pagans considered to be the birthday of the Sun. In 440 A.D., the church arbitrarily assigned this date as the birth of Jesus to accommodate the heathens. Instead of celebrating the birth of Jesus at the Jewish feast of Tabernacles, the most likely time of His birth, the church chose to paganize the date. No wonder, that in times past, Christians were forbidden to celebrate Christmas.

The Romans set aside a special day each week to worship the Sun. They called it the "day of the Sun." We know it as Sunday. The state decreed that Sunday would be set aside as a holiday to worship the Christian god. Thus, the special day of worship was changed from Saturday to Sunday.

The pagan Gentile calendar was adopted by the church rather that the Jewish biblical calendar. The church not

How the Cross Became a Sword

only honors the Sun god on Sunday, but the Moon goddess on Monday and a host of other ancient gods including Tiu (Tuesday), Woden (Wednesday), Thor (Thursday), Frigg (Friday), and Saturn (Saturday).

A triumphant Constantine enforced these new decrees by the sword of the State. He established anti-Semitic polices and declared that contempt for the Jews and separation from them was the only proper Christian attitude. By 339 A.D., it was considered a crime to convert to Judaism. This action by Constantine was a dark preview of future Christian-Jewish relations.

It was not only considered a crime to convert to Judaism, but Jews who acknowledged Jesus as their Messiah also had to renounce their Jewishness and convert to the Gentile brand of Christianity. This is how the absurd idea began that Jews who accepted Jesus as their Messiah were no longer Jewish.

In his book, *Restoring the Jewishness of the Gospel*, David Stern gives the following profession from the Church of Constantinople that was required of Jews who accepted Jesus as their Messiah.

> "I renounce all customs, rites, legalisms, unleavened breads and sacrifices of lambs of the Hebrews, and all the other feasts of the Hebrews, sacrifices, prayers, aspersions, purifications, sanctifications and propitiations, and fasts, and new moons, and Sabbaths, and superstitions, and hymns

and chants and observances and synagogues, and the food and drink of the Hebrews.

"In one word, I renounce absolutely everything Jewish, every law, rite and custom - and if afterwards I shall wish to deny and return to Jewish superstition, or shall be found eating with Jews, or feasting with them, or secretly conversing and condemning the Christian religion instead of openly confuting them and condemning their vain faith, then let the trembling of Cain and the leprosy of Gehazi cleave to me, as well as the legal punishments to which I acknowledge myself liable.

"And may I be anathema in the world to come, and may my soul be set down with Satan and the devils." (David Stern, *Restoring the Jewishness of the Gospel* (Jerusalem: The Jewish New Testament Publications, 1988), page 8).

The institutional church merged with the State and tragically became the bride of Constantine. The Roman State/Church considered itself to be the kingdom of God combining the political and military might of Constantine with Origen's allegorical interpretation of Scripture. One only has to visit Rome and Vatican City to see the imperialistic nature of this State/Church wedding.

The church was soon flooded with pagans who embraced the new Christian religion but never had a personal relationship with Jesus as their Lord and Savior.

How the Cross Became a Sword

They outwardly professed to be Christians in order to gain favor with the Emperor and advance themselves in the Roman world.

This changed the nature and whole character of the church. These non-believers brought their hate against the Jews with them into this new Christian faith. They didn't change gods; they just changed religions.

It was only a matter of time until their hatred of the Jews was manifested by anti-Semitic declarations and actions from the Roman church and government which were essentially one and the same.

During this fourth century, relations between the Christian religious organization and the Jews began to deteriorate. They finally broke in the fifth century with the Roman State/Church viewing the Jews as second-class citizens who were to be forever marked and branded as outcasts from the normal order and decencies of society.

This early anti-Semitic policy of the powerful Roman State/Church laid the foundation for the future of the Jews as they would experience unbelievable suffering and persecution for the next 1500 years.

As the Christian faith spread, more and more countries came under the influence of the Roman church. However, like Rome, many people in these countries accepted Christianity without knowing Jesus personally and experiencing a new life in Him. All they did was to change religions. They continued the anti-Jewish attitudes and policies that came out of the Roman world.

The Crusades

One of the darkest hours for the Jews was during the period of the Crusades. The Crusades were military expeditions conducted under the authority and with the blessings of the church. Their purpose was to recover the Holy Land from the Moslems and stop the spread of Islam. These "Christian" Crusades took place during the eleventh, twelfth and thirteenth centuries.

Although some of the Crusaders were sincere (but misguided) Christians, many more were these same evil-hearted men who were Christian in name only. The Crusades gave them an opportunity to kill and plunder with impunity in the name of God while having their sins forgiven by the Pope.

The Crusaders not only hated the Moslems, but they also hated the Jews. During their conquest of the Holy Land, which was a failure, they savagely butchered thousands of Jews. This was all done under the "banner of the cross and in the name of Christ."

When the Crusaders finally reached Jerusalem, their swords were bathed in blood. They killed the Moslems and herded the Jews into the synagogue. As they sang, "Christ, We Adore Thee," they set fire to the synagogue and burned the Jews alive who were inside. To the Christian church, this slaughter was a just and splendid judgment of God on the unbelievers. To the Jews, it was another example of Christian hate and murder which was to continue over the next centuries.

Anti-Semitism

It was also in the twelfth century that a new charge was leveled against the Jews. This was the charge of *ritual murder*. The charge was that, each year at Passover, the Jews would kill a Christian boy and use his blood in the Passover ritual. This always brought violent mob action against the local Jewish population. There were numerous similar charges against the Jews that were related to the sacraments or ordinances of the church. These too always led to mob violence against the Jews, all in the name of Christ.

As a way of further degrading the Jew, his Gentile lords, from time to time, forced all Jews to wear badges or distinctive clothing which would readily identify them as Jews. In some countries the badge was a yellow "O" similar to the yellow star later used by the Nazi Germans.

The Jews were also forced to live in restricted areas called ghettos. This was done so the "Christian" Gentiles would not have to come into contact with and be contaminated by these "sub-human creatures." It was this attitude that Hitler played on to justify his mass murder of the Jews.

As incredible as it sounds, the Jews were even blamed for the horrible plague that devastated Europe in 1347-1350. It was estimated that this plague, known as the black death, killed approximately one-fourth of Europe's population. Because the Jews practiced better hygiene, they were not as susceptible to the plague as the Gentiles.

The people, needing to have someone to blame for their torment, turned their wrath against the Jews. They accused the Jews of poisoning the wells. Unruly mobs were turned loose on the Jews. Before the plague ended, thousands of Jews were killed and hundreds of Jewish communities completely annihilated.

The Inquisition

The inquisition came next. If you are an American, you remember 1492 as the year that Columbus discovered our great country. Something else happened that year which you may not have learned about in school.

The *Spanish Inquisition* (fifteenth and sixteenth century) was one of the most terrible periods in all of church history. During this period, the leaders of the "Christian" religion tortured and murdered tens of thousands of true Christians who were falsely accused of being heretics. And in their passion for blood, the

How the Cross Became a Sword

Inquisitors also insanely killed hundreds of thousands of Jews. Again, this was all done in the name of Christ. Are you beginning to see why the Jews are intimidated by the name of Christ and feel threatened by the cross and "so-called" Christians?

The inquisition was especially perilous for the Jews in Spain and Portugal. While Columbus was discovering America, Ferdinand and Isabella, at the insistence of the church, began a systematic scheme that brought great suffering on the Jews. They gave the Jews the choice of forced baptism (which is no baptism at all) or exile. If they accepted baptism, the Jews had to renounce their Jewishness. If they refused to be baptized, their property was confiscated and sold to the highest bidder.

Perhaps it was these funds which Ferdinand and Isabella used to finance Columbus's trip? The Jews were either burned alive at the stake or forced to leave the country in conditions that only the hardiest were able to survive. The Jews naturally associated this persecution with Christianity.

Luther - Theologian Of The Holocaust

The reformation of the 1500's brought a needed breath of fresh air to the church. Although the reformers read the Bible in its literal sense, they continued to use the allegorical method of interpreting the Scriptures regarding the relationship of the church to the Jewish people and the prophetic Scriptures concerning end-time events.

In 1523, Martin Luther wrote a pamphlet entitled, *That Christ Was Born a Jew*. He harshly criticized the Catholic Church for presenting a pagan brand of Christianity to the Jews. He expressed empathy for Jews and said, "If I had been a Jew and had seen such fools and blockheads teach the Christian faith, I should rather have turned into a pig than become a Christian."

Tragically, Luther turned against the Jews and wrote two pamphlets attacking them in 1542 and 1543. He proposed that Jewish schools and synagogues be burned, and that Jews be transferred to community settlements (ghettos). He sought to confiscate all Jewish literature he considered to be blasphemous and prohibit rabbis to teach on pain of death. He suggested that Jews be denied safe conduct while traveling in order to prevent the spread of Judaism. He urged that their wealth be taken from them and used to support new converts to Christianity. He taught that Jews should be forced to do manual labor as a form of penance.

Luther's pen was dipped in poison and his writings contain some of the most malicious language ever used against the Jewish people. Luther was not only the theologian of the reformation, but his ideas and writings would by used by Hitler for "Christian" justification of the holocaust. Luther's final comment on the Jews was, "We are at fault for not slaying them."

Thank God that now some leaders in the Evangelical Lutheran Church in America have agreed finally to issue a statement repudiating Luther's words and apologize to the Jews for their past anti-Semitisim. This is an important example that all church organizations should follow in expressing repentance and true Christian love for the Jewish people.

The Russian Pogroms

As we continue on in this broad sweep of Christian-Jewish relations, we come to the latter period of the nineteenth century. The setting is in eastern Europe. Millions of Jews had earlier fled there from the West to escape persecution. Poland became a refuge for them. They found favor with the Polish rulers who gave them some measure of autonomy and enabled them to live without the constant threat of persecution. The Jews felt safe, and old fears begin to wane.

Yet, the trail of tears was not over for them. Russia began to flex her muscles and conquer border states including parts of Poland, Romania and other eastern European countries where there were large Jewish communities. Russia suddenly found herself with an unwanted population of millions of Jews.

Following the example of previous nations, Russian leaders used the Jews as a scapegoat for their internal difficulties. Their solution to this "Jewish problem" was forced conversion for one-third, emigration for another third and starvation for the last third. The Russian word "pogrom," which means destruction, was the name given to this formal persecution against the Jews that took place from 1881-1921 with the tacit approval of the church. The Jews fled back to the west right into Hitler's ovens.

The Holocaust

"The final solution of the Jewish Problem!" That's what Hitler called it. The Jews call it the "Holocaust." This was Hitler's plan for mass murder as the means to completely exterminate the Jews from the face of the earth. He almost did it, but God would preserve a remnant.

Germany had been devastated by World War I. They needed someone to blame for all their problems. Hitler pointed to the Jew. He began organized persecution against them immediately after he took office in 1933. Christians and Jews alike were herded into concentration camps. In 1939, these concentration camps were turned into "death camps."

As Hitler expanded his rule throughout Europe, he shipped Jews by the trainloads from their homelands to these camps. These death factories were so efficient that some of them could mass murder 25,000 human beings every day.

The Jews were stripped of their clothes and herded into gas chambers they thought were shower rooms. When the room was full, the doors were shut, and the people were gassed to death. Afterwards, workers removed gold teeth and wedding rings to be melted down into gold bars. Women's hair was cut and used in the manufacture of cloth and mattresses. Body fat was used to make inexpensive soap. Then after the bodies were cremated, the ashes were used for fertilizer.

The Jewish population in Europe in 1939 was about nine million. Hitler reduced it to three million. The horror of the Holocaust finally awakened the Jew to the fact that the world did not want him. There was no place safe for him to live except in his own homeland. As horrible as this demonic-inspired torture was, God used it to put the desire in the Jewish heart to return to his ancient land in fulfillment of Bible prophecy.

Of course, neither Hitler nor his murdering thugs were Christians, but in the Jewish mind, they represented "Christian" Europe. The question the Jewish people still ask today is, *"Where were the Christians during the Holocaust?"*

There were many Christians who risked their lives to help the Jewish people during the holocaust. Yet, the great majority assisted the Nazis in their murder of the Jews.

How the Cross Became a Sword

As hard as it is to believe, there is a movement today to deny the Holocaust ever happened. General Dwight Eisenhower (later President Eisenhower) anticipated this might happen. He entered Ohrdruf death camp on April 12, 1945, and inspected the camp to witness the Nazi atrocities for himself. He later wrote it was his duty to be in a position to testify first hand about these things in case there ever grew up at home the belief that the stories of Nazi brutality were just propaganda.

I urge all Americans to visit the United States Holocaust Museum in Washington, D.C. to see for yourselves. If in Israel, visit Yad Vashem in Jerusalem.

It is this writer's conviction that the world is building towards another Holocaust. Jesus said in Luke 21:24 that Jerusalem would be under Gentile domination until the "times of the Gentiles" be fulfilled. When the Jews took control of Jerusalem in 1967, it was the beginning of the end of the times of the Gentiles. This is why the Gentile nations are crumbling. *Their day is over!*

As the Gentile nations continue to decline, they will try in vain to establish stability and restore their countries to their former days of glory. In desperation, they will elect radical nationalistic parties that will promise to relieve the suffering of its citizens and re-establish the nation. *These ultra-nationalistic governments will blame the Jews for all their problems.* This is already happening in Russia. Vladimir Zhirinovsky's extremist nationalistic party placed first in Russia's parliamentary elections with nearly 25 percent of the vote.

I believe America will continue to crumble and probably have a financial collapse. *Although America has been a safe haven for the Jews, I do not believe this will be true in the near future.* I believe America will blame the Jews for the financial collapse, and there will be persecution of Jews and true Christians in America.

I strongly urge the Jews in Russia and America to make Aliyah (return to Israel) while you can. God is judging these nations. They will blame you for their suffering.

Don't be like the Jews in Germany who said "it couldn't happen here." *Don't be caught in another Holocaust!* Leave the "fleshpots" of America! Return to Zion! Return to the God of Abraham, Isaac and Jacob. Fulfill your God-given destiny to be a light to the nations! This is your high calling!

To Jewish people who might read these words, I know you don't want to hear them. I know they are not pleasant words. It breaks my heart to write them. I do not say them to hurt you. I do not say them to frighten you. To the contrary, I say them to you as a loving warning and encouragement. The best is yet to come for you but not among the Gentile nations.

To paraphrase a Holocaust victim, I have told you this, not to weaken you, but to strengthen you. Now it is up to you!

Anti-Zionism

Now that the Jewish people are being gathered to their ancient land, anti-Semitism has disguised itself as *anti-Zionism.* "Israel bashing" not only comes from the Arabs, but also from the "Christian" nations and many leaders in the church.

The persecution the Jewish people have experienced the last 2,000 years has been horrifying. As we have seen, much of this persecution has come from the Christian church. I wish I could say it was over. Unfortunately, a spirit of anti-Semitism lies deep in the hearts of many nominal Gentile believers and "churchgoers."

As we have now entered into the time to favor Zion(Ps. 102:12-16), Satan is once again stirring up hate against the Jews and Israel. This spirit of anti-Semitism/anti-Zionism is not just coming from the world but also from church leaders. *There are many "Origenists" in the pulpit today.*

Today, this "new understanding" is called Replacement Theology, Kingdom Now, Dominion, Restoration, or something similar. These teachings rely heavily on the Origen-Augustinian view of the kingdom of God.

There is certainly a measure of truth in these teachings. We are called to live out the principles of the kingdom of God in our lives today. As the Lord Jesus rules and reigns in us, we are able to walk in wholeness and exercise His authority over Satan. We are able to live an abundant Christian life in this world. The kingdom of God has come, in part, in the spiritual realm. But it will also come literally in its fullness.

We misunderstand the Bible if we emphasize only one realm of the kingdom of God. If we focus only on the spiritual realm of the kingdom of God, we will miss its literal aspects and have a tendency to spiritualize it entirely. Likewise, if we only consider the literal realm of the kingdom, we will miss its present reality for our lives today and relegate all of it to the future. *What is needed is a balance recognizing that both aspects of the kingdom of God (spiritual and literal) are presented in the Bible but without the extreme positions just stated.*

The relationship of the church to Israel and the Jewish people has always caused a major division in the church. This division will grow wider and deeper in the near future. A number of well-respected church leaders are following in the footsteps of Luther.

Jesus said a tree is known by its fruit (Matt. 7:16-20). The fruit of the teaching that the church has replaced Israel is a prideful arrogance and hatred towards the Jewish people that is clearly contrary to God's Word and true Christian character.

Paul expressed it with these words in his letter to the believers in Rome, "I say then, has God cast away His people? Certainly not! ... do not boast against the branches (the Jews). But if you do boast, remember that you (the Gentiles) do not support the root, but the root supports you" (Rom. 11:1, 18).

How can a Gentile claim to love Jesus, who is a Jew, while at the same time, hate the Jewish people? An unknown author expressed this contradiction with these words:

"How odd of God to choose the Jew! But not as odd as those who choose the Jewish God, and hate the Jew!"

The Christian Response

As Christians, we must examine our hearts and ask God to take away any hatred we may have towards the Jewish people. We must repent of the past sins of the church (our sins) and then go to the Jewish community in our neighborhoods asking forgiveness. We must determine to take our stand with the Jewish people in the days ahead and support and encourage them with our prayers and deeds of loving kindness.

Finally, as God calls the Jewish people from the Gentile nations to return to their ancient land, we must help them in whatever way possible regardless of what it may cost us. This is the true context of the teaching Jesus gave regarding His judgment on the Gentiles recorded in the book of Matthew.

How the Cross Became a Sword

Jesus instructed the righteous Gentiles " 'Come, you blessed of My Father, inherit the kingdom prepared for you from the foundations of the world: for I was hungry and you gave Me food; I was thirsty and you gave Me drink; I was a stranger and you took Me in; I was naked and you clothed Me; I was sick and you visited Me; I was in prison and you came to Me.'

"Then the righteous will answer Him saying, 'Lord, when did we see You hungry and feed You, or thirsty and give You drink? When did we see You a stranger and take You in, or naked and clothe You? Or when did we see You sick, or in prison, and come to You?'

"And the King will answer and say to them, 'Assuredly, I will say to you, inasmuch as you did it to one of the least of these My brethren, you did it to Me' " (Matt. 25:34-40).

REFERENCES

Booker, Richard. *Blow the Trumpet in Zion*, Shippensburg: Destiny Image, 1985.

Brown, Michael. *Our Hands are Stained with Blood*, Shippensburg: Destiny Image, 1992.

Eusebius. *The History of the Church*, New York: Barnes and Noble, 1965.

Gruber, Daniel. *The Church and the Jews: The Biblical Relationship*, Springfield: General Council of the Assemblies of God, 1992.

Juster, Dan and Intrater, Keith. *Israel, the Church and the Last Days,* Shippensburg: Destiny Image, 1990.

Juster, Dan. *Jewish Roots*, Rockville: DAVAR, 1986.

Perowne, Stewart, *Caesars and Saints: The Rise of the Christian State*, New York: Barnes and Noble, 1992.

Roth, Sid. *Time is Running Short,* Shippensburg: Destiny Image, 1990.

Shanks, Hershel. *Christianity and Rabbinic Judaism*, Washington: Biblical Archaeology Society, 1992.

Stern, David. *Restoring the Jewishness of the Gospel*, Jerusalem: Jewish New Testament Publications, 1988.

Wilson, Marvin. *Our Father Abraham*, Grand Rapids: Eerdmans and Dayton: Center for Judaic-Christian Studies, 1989.

BOOK AND TAPE CATALOG

The Miracle of the Scarlet Thread

This is one of the most profound books ever written on the blood atonement through Jesus Christ. It explains how the First and Second Testaments are woven together by the scarlet thread of the blood covenant to tell one complete story through the Bible. This is a world-wide bestselling classic. *Over 100,000 copies in print!*

Blow the Trumpet in Zion

This book explains the dramatic and fascinating story of the Jewish people, Israel and the nations in prophecy. It is *one of the most informative books available* relating Bible prophecy to world history and current and future events as they revolve around God's covenant plan for the Jewish people and Israel.

Jesus in the Feasts of Israel

This is a study of the Old Testament feasts showing how they pointed to Jesus and their *personal* and *prophetic* significance for today's world. The reader also discovers how the feasts represents seven steps in the believer's walk with God.

How the Cross Became a Sword

This publication explains the events that separated Christianity from its Jewish roots and established anti-Semitism as official church doctrine. It then gives an *excellent overview* of the tragic history of Christian-Jewish relations directly linking modern replacement theology to the first Christian seminary in Alexandria, Egypt.

Islam, Christianity and Israel

This publication reveals shocking information about the life of Mohammed and the background, teachings and practices of Islam. It also explains how Islam differs from Christianity and is threatening to conquer the West. The reader learns "*what they won't tell you on the evening news*" about the conflict between the Arabs and the Jews and how the conflict will end.

BOOK ORDER FORM

Sounds of the Trumpet - IHCS
4747 Research Forest Dr Ste 180-330
Woodlands, TX 77381
www.rbooker.com shofarprb@aol.com
Ph: 936-441-2171 Fax: 936-494-1999

To order books by Sounds of the Trumpet, check the appropriate box(es) below to: Sounds of the Trumpet, Houston, Tx. 77070.

- ❏ Please send me ____ copy(ies) of *The Miracle of the Scarlet Thread*. I have enclosed $7.95 for each book ordered (includes shipping).

- ❏ Please send me ____ copy(ies) of *Blow the Trumpet in Zion*. I have enclosed $7.95 for each book ordered (includes shipping).

- ❏ Please send me ____ copy(ies) of *Jesus in the Feasts of Israel*. I have enclosed $7.95 for each book ordered (includes shipping).

- ❏ Please send me ____ copy(ies) of *How the Cross Became A Sword*. I have enclosed $5.95 for each book ordered (includes shipping).

- ❏ Please send me ____ copy(ies) of *Islam, Christianity and Israel*. I have enclosed $5.95 for each book ordered (includes shipping).

Name _____
Address _____
City _____
State _____ Zip _____

Foreign orders please send an additional $2.00 per book ordered in U. S. funds only for surface mail.

TAPE ORDER FORM

To order appropriate Sounds of 77070.

Sounds of the Trumpet - IHCS
4747 Research Forest Dr Ste 180-330
Woodlands, TX 77381
www.rbooker.com shofarprb@aol.com
Ph: 936-441-2171 Fax: 936-494-1999

heck the below to: ton, Tx.

All tapes are $5.00 each (includes shipping). Please enclose payment with order. Foreign orders please add an additional $2.00 per tape ordered in U.S. dollars only for surface mail.

- ❑ Why God Chose the Jews
- ❑ Israel and Nations in Prophecy
- ❑ Time to Favor Zion
- ❑ Times of the Gentiles
- ❑ The Messianic Kingdom
- ❑ How the Cross Became A Sword
- ❑ Islam, Christianity and Israel
- ❑ How to Recognize the Jewish Messiah
- ❑ Israel or Palestine: Whose Land is it?
- ❑ Expressing Christian Love to the Jews
- ❑ Survey of the Feasts
- ❑ Celebrating the Feasts in the Church

Name _____

Address _____

City _____

State _____ Zip _____